MEET THE REAL ME

KIDS ACROSS AMERICA TELL THEIR STORIES

Compiled by Peggy Gavan
Illustrated by Janice Kinnealy

Troll Associates

Library of Congress Cataloging-in-Publication Data

Meet the real me / written by kids; compiled by Peggy Gavan;
  illustrated by Janice Kinnealy.
     p.   cm.
   Summary: Students in grades two through eight describe themselves,
discussing their goals, dreams, talents, and other special
qualities.
   ISBN 0-8167-2939-5 (pbk.)
   1. United States—Biography—Juvenile literature. [1. Children—
United States—Biography—Juvenile literature. 2. Children's
writings, American.] I. Gavan, Peggy. II. Kinnealy, Janice, ill.
CT217.M44 1993
920. '0083—dc20   92-21644

Copyright © 1993 by Troll Associates

All rights reserved. No part of this book may be used or

reproduced in any manner whatsoever without written

permission from the publisher.

Printed in the United States of America.

10 9 8 7 6 5 4 3 2 1

Meet the Real Me!

Everyone in this world is very special! Some people are special because they have unique talents and hobbies, while others may be special because of their family size, hair color, shoe size, or funny habits. We asked you to introduce yourself, and to tell us some of the things that make you the special person — the *real* person — that you are. The response was tremendous!

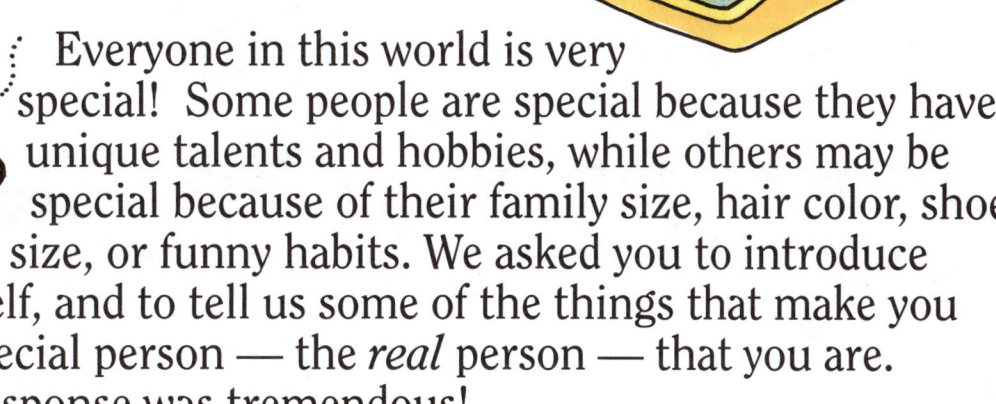

We received thousands of essays, each as unique as the students who wrote them! The very best essays — humorous, serious, poetic — were compiled and put into this book. Each student's name and grade appear next to the essay. And at the back of the book, you'll find an alphabetical list of winners, along with their schools and school addresses.

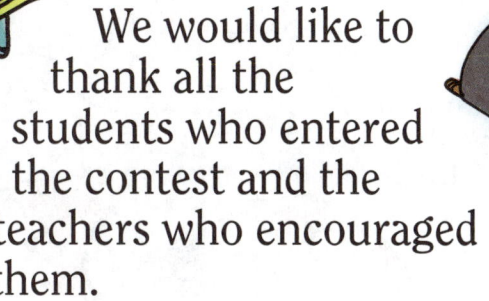

We would like to thank all the students who entered the contest and the teachers who encouraged them.

I'M SOMEONE SPECIAL!

This is a story about one of the billions of people in the world — Dan Annarelli. Born on May 16, 1979, I am 12 years old and presently in seventh grade attending St. Denis School. Playing sports, watching TV, listening to music, playing video games, collecting baseball cards and comic books, spending money, and spending time with my friends are the things I most enjoy. I also have a landscaping business with my friends to make a few extra bucks, and a paper route. I am a very lucky child. I've been blessed with athletic ability, musical ability, intelligence, and a free will. I realize, and I hope that other people do too, that I am a unique person. But I cannot take all the credit. My parents are the best and they've brought me up to be the very best that I can be.

Dan Annarelli
Grade 7

My name is Kelly. I am special in a lot of ways. I feel special when my mom hugs me, and when my sister says, "I love you." When my dad says, "You did good!" I feel very special.

When I do good in school it makes me feel really good. When my sister gives me a kiss, and when my mom and dad tuck me in at night, I know I'm special.

Kelly Barber
Grade 2

If I were 15 years old, I could drive a car. But I'm not. I'm only seven years old. If my name was Robin Hood, I would be famous. I'm not famous, but my mama says I'm very special.

I am David Andrew Cook. I have brown hair. Maybe you would like to meet me someday. I'm a very nice boy and I make a good friend, too.

David Cook
Grade 2

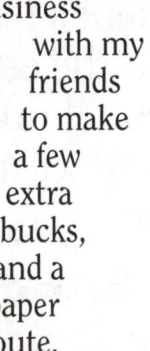

The question of why I am me pops into my head quite often. I've tried to come up with a reasonable answer, but I have not found one yet. I do know, however, that I am special in lots of ways. I am a good athlete and I try my best to do well in academics. My future ambition is to become a lawyer, or an actress.

I may not be as smart as Albert Einstein, and I may not be as pretty as Miss America, but nobody is better at being Kathleen Elizabeth Elia than me!

Katie Elia
Grade 6

My name is Tara Renee Radford, and I will tell you some things that I like about me.

I like my round little tummy and the clothes I wear. I keep myself clean and healthy. I am not too small or too tall. I'm just right. Every time I wake up I say, "Hi, good looking." And I'm especially special because my family loves me!

Tara Radford
Grade 2

What makes me special is that I'm my own self and not what somebody else wants me to be. What also makes me special is my ability to fail as well as succeed. I try to succeed in everything that I do, but if I do fail, I try again and never let my self-confidence go down. I

try my hardest in most things that I do. And I promise myself everyday that I will never drink alcohol, take drugs, or smoke. That's what makes me special.

B.J. Rapp
Grade 7

I am a dark-haired third-grade girl. I have four sisters, but I'm the only one with freckles. I think I am special because I was the one chosen to be named after my grandmother. I never got to meet my grandmother because she died before I was born, but I feel honored to be the one to carry on her name. She would be proud to have someone named after her. That's why I feel special.

Mary Clacko
Grade 3

I am special! I am special because God created me to be on this earth for a reason; to do a certain task like save someone's life, invent a product useful to the world, or discover something new.

I am special because when God created me, he gave me features that no one else has. I am also special because I may have an ability to do something others can't do, like drawing talents or writing talents. I may publish a poem or a best-selling novel!

This is why I, Raymond Eddy, am special to me, my family, and the world.

Raymond Eddy
Grade 6

I've Got Talent

My name is John Theodossiou and I am a ballroom dancer. In competition, I do the samba, waltz, cha-cha, swing, rumba, fox-trot, and tango.

My opinion is that dancing is fun and exciting. Although I usually compete with kids older than me, I still win. So far, my sister Irene and I have won seven first-place awards for waltz, cha-cha, swing, rumba, and tango.

In addition to competing, I also dance for the Easter Seals Charity Ball. Easter Seals is an organization for kids who can't walk. Our slogan is, "We dance so others may walk."

*John Theodossiou
Grade 7*

When I first started jumping double-dutch, I was in the third grade. I wasn't very good. I knew if I wanted to be number one I had to practice and practice. I kept at it, jumping whenever I had the chance, practicing at home and still more at school.

Now I am in the sixth grade and I am considered the best double-dutch jumper in school! I had a goal and I went for it.

Now I know I can do anything I want to do — all I have to do is practice. Being the number-one double-dutch jumper in school makes me one of the happiest girls alive!

*Jeanine Williams
Grade 6*

I really like gardening, but I don't have very good luck with plants. For example, when everyone in the class planted beans, everyone's grew except mine. When my brother and I planted corn, his grew fine. Why didn't mine?

So I decided to buy a plant already full-grown. What could go wrong? It was a perfect idea. I got a very nice rosebush, but it didn't get enough water.

Then one day an odd idea struck me. I would draw a flower! It looked half okay, and it didn't need water.

Every day I drew a new picture and finally I was the best artist in my class!

*Lexy Patterson
Grade 6*

What makes me special? Well, I play the piano, I can almost play the guitar, and I have written four books. My parents think I should

be an artist. My dad says I'm great at wrapping presents!

*Colleen Gerossie
Grade 2*

I think I'm special because I can do lots of sound effects and impressions. My number one impression is Donald Duck sneezing.

I first started to imitate people when I was six. When I started I could only do three or four impressions, but over the years, I have learned to do 60 more impressions.

I can also do awesome sound effects. I first got started doing sound effects when I was four years old. Just name the sound effect, and I can make it!

*Anthony DeFrancesco
Grade 5*

My name is Mary Dalton, and I'd like to tell you what makes me unique. I am unique because I can communicate with deaf people. You might not think this is different, but it is because deaf people use a special language. It is called sign language or Ameslan for short. In this language I don't use my mouth to talk — I use my hands. You would be surprised to see how many different ways there are to sign one word!

My parents taught me sign language when I was very little. I have signed songs on stage for talent shows, and I have signed plays at a local theater. Sign language is very interesting, and I'm glad I learned it.

*Mary Dalton
Grade 7*

I am a special person because I have big ears. I don't like them, but I guess they're just there. Sometimes people call me "Dumbo" or say, "Watch out, the wind is blowing. You might fly away." It really doesn't bother me because I am me.

I'M UNIQUE

My ears make me a special person because they are *my* big ears, and not my mom's, dad's, or yours — and you can't have them!

*Ronda White
Grade 6*

I am a special person because I have white hair. Not many people have white hair. I like white hair because it is different. I think my hair is neat. My hair makes me special.

*Ed Berghorn
Grade 4*

My name is Gurpreet Virk. I am an Indian from India. I look different from other boys in my classroom because I wear a turban on my head. I have long hair, and I wear it in a bun on my head.

I feel like I am treated like an idiot because people make fun of my turban. I like my turban and I'm not going to cut my hair because the men in my culture wear turbans. I like me just the way I am.

*Gurpreet Virk
Grade 3*

I am special because I have red hair. Being a redhead is not always a joy, but it makes me feel extra special because I'm redheaded and most of the world isn't. When anybody talks about my red hair, I just say, "This is the way God made me — redheaded and special." After telling anyone this, I feel happy that I have just stood up for my rights as a redhead. By now, every redhead should know that it's okay to have red hair.

*Kena Crabtrey
Grade 6*

People say I look like a monkey. I think it is very funny. Most people started to call me a monkey when I was a baby. People said I looked like a baby chimpanzee. When I was little, I thought they were making fun of me, but I have grown to like it now. I think it is cool.

I love monkeys. They are my favorite animals. I am special because I look like a monkey.

Steve Passaloukos
Grade 5

I am different from most people in the world because I have two different colored eyes. One eye is blue and some people think the other is brown. Others think it is green. Whatever color it is, when I grow up and get my driver's license, I guess I'll have to list my eye color as "mixed." This can be very confusing, but I think it is special.

Jennifer Kimble
Grade 2

The real me is an outgoing, fun-loving, kind, and caring type of guy. I have thick hair, big brown eyes, good health, and a great personality.

When some people look at me, they want to pick on me about my eyes and hair. I don't like it, but I live with it. To them, my eyes are big and look like bugs' eyes, but to me, they're all the better to see with. To them, my hair looks funny on my head, but I don't care. I try to ignore people when they pick on me, but it's hard. People see me in a totally different light than I do. All I see is an outgoing, fun-loving, kind, and caring type of guy.

Blaine Findley
Grade 8

The Athletic Me!

Football is in my blood. My father is a coach, and I've been around high school football players all my life. I play with my brother and I always win. Sometimes I play at lunch time with my friends. I'm also planning to play on the high school and Florida State University football teams.

The real me is a future center for the New York Giants. I'm quick, tough, athletic, and love football. There's no doubt about it, I'm a good football player. And if I get to play on a team, I might live out my dream.

*Vinnie DiStefano
Grade 4*

Soccer is a very big kick to me. My favorite sport is soccer. I play for a team that travels. It is special to me because my mom is the club manager. The tournaments we've been to so far have been located in North Carolina, Georgia, and South Carolina.

My goal is to play high school soccer and get a scholarship to play college soccer. When I graduate I want to play professional soccer for the U.S. World Cup team.

*Ronnie Burbage
Grade 5*

The real me is someone with a dream to one day become a professional gymnast. My family encourages me to become a gymnast. I take lessons with a coach and I hope to make it to the Junior Olympics. My coach will help me reach this goal.

I hope my dream comes true someday. Keep trying, and yours will, too.

*Heather Holman
Grade 5*

I feel that I am a very unique person in many ways. Of course I enjoy the normal things — basketball, bikes, music, and reading — but my real love is go-cart racing.

I have been competing

in this sport for four years. I have traveled to many different states and competed in my first national event last season. This past season was my most successful so far. I was the Tri-State Rookie Champion and the Blankethill Box Stock Junior Champion. I feel that I am a good driver because I use my brains instead of just a lead foot. My mom and dad always tell me, "Do well in school, and you can do anything that you put your mind to in life!"

I will continue to practice hard for everything I do — my racing, my basketball, and most of all, my school work. My goals for the future are to be an engineer and to race on the Winston Cup circuit. Between now and then I would like to win a lot more races and improve my school work. I feel that I am a pretty special kid.

Kevin Schaeffer
Grade 7

As one of the 10 junior high cheerleaders for Marengo Academy, I attend a cheerleading camp every year to learn and compete. I have been a junior high cheerleader for two years now, and I love it. I enjoy meeting people, and cheerleading gives me the perfect opportunity to do so at games and camps.

Being an athletic person, cheerleading and gymnastics have always come easily to me. But even though I enjoy cheerleading and gymnastics the most, I have thought about my future and like the idea of attending the University of Alabama and one day becoming a lawyer.

Kelley Jacobs
Grade 8

"**K**ristin!" my skating coach yells to me on an early Friday morning, telling me to bend my knees so I can jump higher in my loop jump. I don't know what inspired me, but I'm glad I started. I was five years old when I signed up for a learn-to-skate program. Now I'm thirteen, and I'm still skating. I guess it's because skating is the one sport I love, and nobody is forcing me to do the one thing I love to do.

When I'm skating in an ice show and when I'm practicing, there are many different things to do on the ice, such as jumps and spins. I get scared when I have to skate in front of people, but I overcome the fear by just going out on the ice and doing what I have to do. I will be skating in my first competition this year, and I am really scared. But I just have to get out there and do it.

To me, skating is not just hard work, but it is also a really fun sport. The speed you pick up makes you feel like you're gliding on air. I guess that's why I like it so much.

Kristin Siple
Grade 8

From Faraway Lands

One of the things I love to do is fly. I think flying to exotic places in the world like Hong Kong, Singapore, and Kuala Lumpur make me unique because I know about so many different cultures.

I lived more than eight of my 12 years of life in Indonesia, which is a country in Southeast Asia. Twice a year, at Christmas and summer vacation, I flew home to the United States. The longest flight I was ever on was 15 hours long, and I loved every minute of it.

Now I live in Texas, but I go back to Jakarta, Indonesia, to visit my old home and my old friends who still live there. It was an adventure flying around the world, but I enjoy being at home in one place. I think that I am very lucky to live the life I have. And that's the real me.

*Justin Reyburn
Grade 6*

My name is Nadhira Michelle Suhaila Yogarajah. I am a twelve-year-old girl who was born in Kuwait. Although I was born in Kuwait, I am a Sri-Lankan National. My family and I were in the United States on vacation when the invasion took place in Kuwait. My family has decided to remain here, although we find the lifestyle very different from what we were used to before.

My hobbies are ballet, swimming, and playing the piano. I started swimming when I was seven years old, and before coming to the United States, I won a bronze and silver medal in swimming. I am so sorry I left all these medals in Kuwait when I came here.

One of my favorite interests is traveling by plane. I have visited Paris, Sri Lanka, India, Lourdes, England, Florida, Canada, Kuwait, and Thailand. I like Thailand the best because it is a beautiful, calm, quiet place.

*Nadhira Yogarajah
Grade 7*

I live in Japan, near the United States Navy Base in Yokosuka. In my neighborhood, there are many poor children. They live in orphanages. I try to give them my old toys so they will be happy. Sometimes I help my mom bake cookies and decorate them and send them to Japanese-Americans who are nice to know.

Michael Austin
Grade 2

My name is Vlad Babadzhanov. I know this name is very hard to pronounce, but what can I do? I would change my last name, but it is all I have left of my Russian heritage.

I came to this country with my family two years ago. Now I am becoming an American and I am proud of it. I try to study hard in school. I like learning new things. It is not always easy for me. Russian and American together — that's me.

Vlad Babadzhanov
Grade 6

Hi, my name is Patricia. I am from El Salvador, but I have been living in Guatemala for one and a half years. I am 10 years old and I study at Colegio Maya.

My language is Spanish, but I know a lot of English as you can see. In the school that I go to we have to speak English, but most of the time my friends and I speak Spanish.

I love to dance when I have free time, but I have a little problem — I am very shy when I dance in front of people. Now that I am practicing a little more, the shyness is going out of me.

Patricia Suriano
Grade 5

My name is Jennifer and I am eight years old. I was born in South Korea, in a city called Seoul.

I came to the United States on March 29, 1983, when I was three months old. My new parents gave me the name Jennifer Marie Saxe.

I have several interesting hobbies. Two of my favorite hobbies are collecting stamps and coins. I also like to collect shells. I also enjoy listening to records. Some of my favorite groups are the Beach Boys, the Carpenters, and Peter, Paul, and Mary. Now I am learning how to play the cello, too.

Jennifer Saxe
Grade 4

Just Me and My Imagination

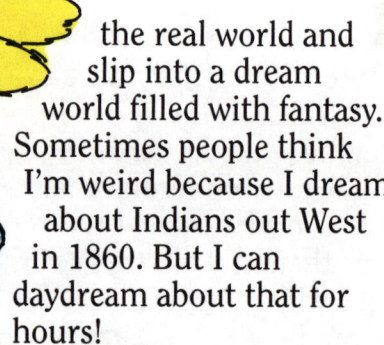

My name is Moses and I am a bird lover. I have a bird named Polly. Polly is a parakeet.

I am a very imaginative kid. Sometimes I imagine I am a bird of prey. I swoop and dive. I bring my wings up and level my tail. Other times I pretend I'm soaring fast. But it's hard to imagine how great that must feel. I'd love to be a bird!

Moses Barrett
Grade 2

It's the year 1860. I'm riding a cinnamon-colored mare across a wide prairie with wild dandelions growing freely. The sun is shining brightly, making my mare's coat gleam and shimmer.

Actually, I'm in my math class, daydreaming. We're supposed to be paying attention, but math bores me. I'm always daydreaming when I'm in school. Usually I dream about being with Indians out West in 1860. I just tune out the real world and slip into a dream world filled with fantasy. Sometimes people think I'm weird because I dream about Indians out West in 1860. But I can daydream about that for hours!

Killeen Tracy
Grade 7

The real me is a dog trapped in a boy's body. I was a dog in a past life, but I was reincarnated into Derek Ruud, an average eighth-grader at Grygla Junior High. I have visions of being a dog in my dreams. So now I am living a double life of a 13-year-old during the day and a dog chasing a fire engine at night. I have gone to many experts, and they all say that my dreams of being a dog are a sign that I was once a dog in a past life.

In reality I am not a dog. I'm just an average kid. I have blue eyes and brown hair. I have one brother and one sister. I live a pretty normal life for a teenager.

Derek Ruud
Grade 8

I, Meaghan Burritt, have two sides. One side is just me, a normal sixth-grader with hazel eyes, freckles, brown hair, and wonderful friends and family. The other, imaginative, side is the exciting, but dreamy side.

The exciting, dreamy side wishes I could grow up and be a beautiful, famous model. I would model in New York with a very good photographer. That photographer would be my wonderful handsome husband, who will have short brown hair with deep brown eyes. We will live in a beautiful penthouse and have a wonderful child.

Even though I might not end up being a famous model with a beautiful husband and child living in a beautiful penthouse, I will always be loving and caring about our world and my family.

*Meaghan Burritt
Grade 6*

"It's Tom Cruise. It's Luke Perry! No, it's Dan Mitry!"
I am Dan Mitry, the ultimate stud. Every girl loves me and thinks I am great; however, I am trying to keep it down to 18 girlfriends a week. I am very strong and tall. I have blond hair and I drive a Rolls Royce and a Lamborghini.

"Wow, what a good dream!" I say to myself.

The real me is not too tall, not too strong, and has brown hair. I have a big, flat nose and big feet. I am not very popular and girls don't really like me. But I am a good student and I am very good at sports. As you can see, I am not really a superstar, nor am I a stud. However, I am really not unhappy with the way I am.

*Daniel Mitry
Grade 7*

When I Grow Up...

I am special because no one is like me, and because no one can think like me and do what I can do.

When I grow up, I would like to be a teacher, mother, driver, nurse, artist, and astronaut. I want to be an astronaut because I want to be the first person to go to Mars. I want to be a teacher because I want to teach second grade. I think teaching second grade will be fun.

I want to be an artist because I think that I draw well. And I want to be a nurse because I want to help people stay alive and I want to help the doctors who help people have babies.

I would like to be a mother because I do not want to be alone. And I want to be a driver because I want to go to New York to see how it looks and to see how big it really is.

Fifi Wang
Grade 2

I think there is too much pollution. Pollution kills too many animals! When we grow up and have children, there will be smoke everywhere in the air if we keep polluting!

When I grow up, I'm going to make a club for removing pollution. I'm going to build a machine that recycles almost everything in the world! I'm talking about recycling not only things like paper, bottles, and cans, but also clothes, cars, and batteries! I'm going to ask people to participate, or it won't work.

Ricky Lyman
Grade 4

I would like to grow up to become a famous children's author and an illustrator. I think I would enjoy writing and drawing for kids of all ages. I would like to write and draw like Dr. Seuss or write novels like Beverly Cleary. I would like to try to win Newbery Awards, too!

If I become an author and illustrator I will try to encourage kids to read more often. I will go to schools in my spare time and see how kids are doing. I know being an author and an illustrator is a big job,

but if I keep on trying for it, it will come to me!

Tram Le
Grade 5

My dream is to be a lifeguard when I am older because I like to swim and dive in the water. But I don't want to be a lifeguard just for fun. The water is dangerous. If someone does not know how to swim, they could drown. I would like to be a lifeguard to save someone's life, like a lifeguard once saved my life when I almost drowned a long time ago. I hope my dream comes true.

Arturo Maldonado
Grade 5

I am a girl and I am skinny and tall. I am seven years old. I have black hair. I like cars and I like to run. I also like to read.
When I grow up, I want to have 20 kids and get married, too.

Willimena Bemah
Grade 2

When I grow up, I want to be a store person. I will help people that need help finding items. I will ring up the toys, fruits, and vegetables. I will help carry people's bags out to the car. I will say, "Have a nice day. Bye, thank you."

Missy Harris
Grade 4

I was born on October 22, 1981, with a head like my grandfather's — bald on the top with a few strands of hair on the sides. I am now 10 years old, and I go to C.G. Credle School.
My dream is to become a track star and travel all over the world. I want to become a track star so I can help pay back my parents for all the years they took care of me.

Taquanica L. Royster
Grade 4

When I Grow Up...

One of my favorite hobbies is making electrical gadgets. I love electricity so much, that my favorite toys were always plugs and wires!

Every time we went shopping, my mom would always find me near a cash register, trying to pull out the plug. (I succeeded many times.) I still drive her crazy at home, as she always finds wires everywhere.

So that's the real me — a future electrical engineer. Thank goodness I wasn't born before electricity was discovered!

*Anthony Koscica
Grade 3*

Who am I? I'm Anne Klein. I know some of you might remember the famous designer, but when my mom named me, Anne Klein wasn't popular.

I would like to be an astro-geologist. An astro-geologist is a person who studies rocks and minerals from outer space. I'm good at science, math, and reading, which will help me reach my goal. I hope to go to Michigan State University to get a doctorate in geology and aerospace — this way, NASA can't refuse me. I'd like to go to Mars and live in a colony there. I'd also like to live in Florida or Houston. And sometime in there I would like to get married.

Well, that's me, Anne Klein.

*Anne Klein
Grade 7*

The real me is no one but me. There is only one me — one Rober Alexander Mantilla Santamaria in the world. There is only one Rober who was born on May 12, 1979, in Quito, Ecuador.

One of my main goals is to become a pilot. If I decide to join the Army I will train in air combat skills called dog-fighting. I will fly a combat plane, preferably an F-14 Tomcat, and soar through the sky like mist in the night. My call-sign will be "Bear" because my nickname is Bear.

My other goal, should I choose, is to become a computer

designer. I will become the most creative designer that ever lived. I will design a computer that will have a TV, VCR, 25-bit video game system, and a regular computer all in one screen. I will name this model "Bear 10,000." And this is the real me.

Rober Mantilla
Grade 7

My favorite thing to do is play and take care of babies. They are so soft and tiny. Babies smile all the time. They are really neat.

The real me would make everybody a baby again so all the people in the world would smile, hug, kiss, and like one another. That is why the real me wants to be a mommy when I grow up.

Vanessa Aiello
Grade 2

My name is Justin Blankenship. My hopes and dreams in life are to go to college and then become a preacher. I've wanted to do this since I was three years old.

I would like to grow up, get married, and settle down to a nice little family and have a peaceful life. One of my goals is to do a little mission work around the world. I know that there are a lot of hurting people in the world. I would like to help them in the future.

Justin Blankenship
Grade 5

I am unique because my parents are deaf. It is not very hard for me, but it takes time to get used to it. I try to help my parents any way I possibly can by interpreting, making calls for them, and helping other people understand them.

Once I get out of school and college, I plan to become a teacher for the deaf, teaching sign language and speech therapy. I want to follow in my parents' footsteps and be a useful person by helping those less fortunate.

Lisa Parulis
Grade 7

Hi, I'm James Hinkle. I live in Aurora, Colorado, but I was born in Socouro, New Mexico. I am the captain and goalie of my soccer team, an excellent skier, enrolled in honors reading and spelling, and a candidate for class president. My favorite foods include pizza, hot dogs, all soups, all Far Eastern foods, milk shakes, malts, ice cream, chocolate, French bread, Italian food and Mexican food. I hate most vegetables save iceberg lettuce.

I am 11 years old and love world affairs. I want to be a pro skier, pro soccer player, and then a five-star general. I'd also like to be Secretary of Defense, Secretary of War, Supreme Court Justice, and the President.

James Hinkle
Grade 6

The Poetic Me

If you're Pisces, or Libra, or Taurus,
just join along and sing the chorus.
　I'm special, I'm special, look and see,
meet the real me!
　I'm Sagittarius, maybe you're Aquarius!
　Everyone's special, 'specially me!
　I'm very dutiful, people say I'm beautiful.
　I love to sing, to unicorns I love to cling.
　I like to make friends, collect odds and ends.
　'Cause I'm special, I'm special, look and see,
meet the real me!

*Gwuinifer Kenoyer
Grade 5*

I'm me, I'm drug-free, I'm cool, I swim in the pool.
　I seldom hate, I love to skate,

The "Real Me" is a little boy that is small. But I'd rather be a big boy, nice and tall.
　The "Real Me" is missing some teeth, but I'd rather be you, so I could chew some meat.
　The "Real Me" is seven years old. I wish I were eight — then maybe I could date!
　But the "Real Me" is a special boy. How do I know? Because my mom told me so!

*Talton Jett
Grade 2*

If I was a car I would be a sports car, because I really love sports — watching, and playing.
　If I was a vegetable, I would be a celery stick, because I'm slender and healthy.
　If I was a machine, I would be a TV, because I like to entertain people.
　If I was an animal, I would be a hyena, because I love comedy.
　If I was a tree, I would be a Christmas tree to light up the night.
　If I was any color, I would be yellow to light up the day.
　That is the real me.

*Alberto Silva
Grade 8*

If I had to think of myself as a tree, the tree would be a weeping willow. A weeping willow stands tall and proud, but willing to bend in the breeze and stand strong through all kinds of weather. The roots of my weeping willow are strong and grow deep as my family roots.

My branches are long with life. I have made many friendships in the states I have lived in, and those branches hold friendships that I will cherish forever. The shorter, younger branches are my new interests, such as cheerleading, tennis, my church, and my membership in the National Junior Honor Society.

Between these visible branches are those that are hidden in the foliage. Just as my many moods and other interests are hidden, these branches are waiting to be discovered as a new and important part of me.

Misti C. Humphrey
Grade 8

Spencer
Musical, artistic, creative, yet athletic,
Brother of music, Son of nature,
Lover of sports, family, and friends,
Who feels that everyone is created equal, that everything has a meaning, and that everyone has a right to a good education.
Who needs love, care, and space to grow,
Yet fears pain, getting old, and death,
And would like to see respect for one's rights, peace, and no violence,
Resident of Sandy Hook,
Swain

Spencer Swain
Grade 5

Me On The Inside

Most people describe me as a nice girl who is friendly and makes good grades. But sometimes I want to be more than nice — I want to be spectacular, glamorous and amazing. I want to be the REAL me!

The real me *is* spectacular, glamorous and amazing. The real me is a beautiful ballet star. My strong, graceful body moves in time to beautiful music. I wear elegant costumes and white satin toe shoes. My audience is the world and I perform on a stage extended into outer darkness. I'm as light as air, and when I am lifted, I soar into the night sky, glittering with the stars and the full-faced moon. The moon is my goal I dream of reaching.

When I fly I can touch the moon, my dream for an everlasting second. Finally, I can finish my dance among the glittering silver moonbeams. My stage is no longer in front of the world. It is in front of the universe.

The real me is not just a nice girl. The real me can be wonderful. The real me will dance for an eternity on the moon, my dream, my goal.

Melony Clemons
Grade 7

When I stop and really think about who the real me is, I realize that I am a very special and unique person. Even though I don't always like what I see in the mirror, I know that my looks are not the most important thing. The most important thing is who I am inside.

When someone becomes my friend, it's not because I have brown hair or because my name is Lourdes. I'm sure that my friends don't like me because of the way I look, but because they can trust me. They know, that in good times or bad, I'll be there beside them. They like who the "real me" is.

Lourdes Diaz
Grade 8

On the inside, I am a Navy fighter pilot; on the outside, I'm just a kid.

On the inside, I'm a warrior; on the outside, I'm just a fighter.

On the inside, I'm an eagle in flight; on the outside, I'm flying in an airplane.

On the inside, I am Sinbad the Sailor; on the outside, I'm just reading a book.

On the inside, I'm a muscle-man; on the outside, I merely lift weights.

Dan Coburn
Grade 4

Some people call me pint-sized, but in the important ways, I am very big. I am big in the heart and big in the soul and the mind. I'm big in ways so I can do things without somebody with me. I am also able to do many things that tall people cannot do because I am small. I can get things in small places because of my size. So just because I'm small, it doesn't mean a thing. As the saying goes, "Good things come in small packages."

Christine Como
Grade 3

The real me is someone that only my cat has seen. The real me happens after hours, when I close my door and lock out peers, parents, and pressure. The real me sings and dances in front of my mirror, swaying my head from side to side, while the stereo is up full blast. I pretend to be on a stage, in front of thousands! Yet I hope that no one will see me.

The real me is not the teacher's pet, or the brain, or a preppy. The real me is a movie star, a Newbery Award-winning author, a Nobel Peace Prize winner, a track star, a Grammy-winning singer, a hero to everyone.

The real me is someone who matters; someone that everybody likes and hangs around with; someone they can tell secrets to. The real me is not just used and manipulated by others to get what they want. The real me just wants to be left alone, just wants people to stop hurting me, and holding me back.

Bronwen Murray
Grade 7

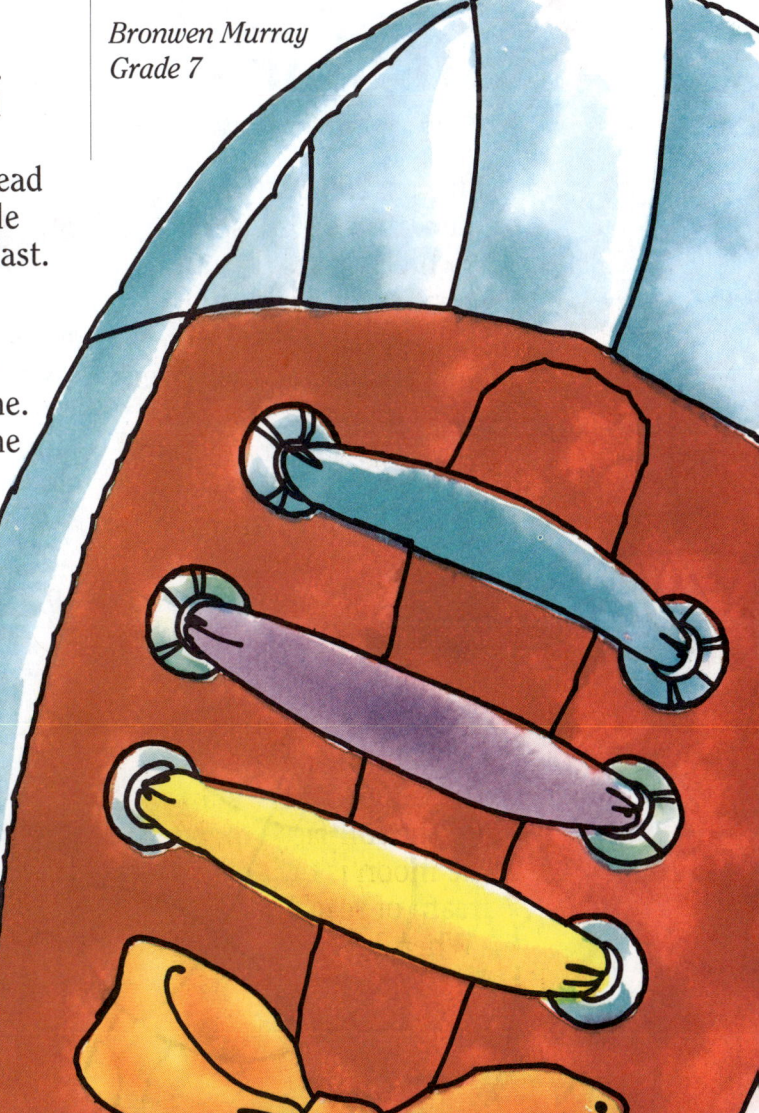

I'm Extra Special!

I know how the Teenage Mutant Ninja Turtles feel, because I'm a bobby-soxer in a half-shell. I wish someone would crack my shell so I could get out, because it is tight and uncomfortable.

I really don't wear a shell — I wear a Milwaukee brace. I wear this brace because I have scoliosis — I have a 290 degree curvature of the spine, which makes the one side of my back higher than the other. My doctor told me I need to wear a brace to straighten my spine or at least keep it from getting worse.

My parents and I do not let scoliosis or my brace keep me from doing the things I enjoy. This summer I attended basketball camp, and I also hope to play Little League basketball.

Even though I sometimes feel like a bobby-soxer in a half-shell, I know when it is time for me to come out of my shell my back will be perfectly straight and I will sit like a graceful model.

Leah Stark
Grade 6

When I was born, I was born without part of my left arm. Now I have to wear a special device called a prosthesis to help me do things like other kids can do.

What I like to do most are sports. My favorite sports are ice hockey and basketball. To play hockey, I have another special device that I use to hold my hockey stick. I also play basketball for my school team.

I am lucky to have friends and family who love me for the way I am.

Joseph Carro
Grade 3

My name is Alan. I am eight years old and blind. I am special because I help my dad cut the grass. I push the lawn mower and I listen to the lawn mower cut the grass. I think it is fun to help my dad. My dad thinks it is fun to cut the grass with me.

Alan Restivo
Grade 2

Do you know what it is like to think you are different from everyone else? I do.

It all started when I was smaller. When everyone else was writing their ABCs and 123s, I was too. But somehow, mine didn't turn out the same, no matter how hard I tried. I knew what they were and could say them, but writing them was different.

The same thing went for my spelling and math. I knew the answers and could spell out loud. I just couldn't put it on paper the right way. I thought I was just stupid.

Thank goodness for parents and teachers who cared. They found out I was dyslexic. With lots of help and practice, I have overcome many obstacles that may have stopped me in my tracks. My writing still isn't perfect, but I don't feel stupid any more.

I feel very blessed because I no longer think I am stupid. I'm now very determined. I also feel very proud and honored, because I made the honor roll last year.

My point is this: You can either just accept things as they are, or you can become determined and change them.

*Don Allen Mitchell
Grade 8*

I am special because of my many traits. One of those traits is my albinism. It makes my hair and skin very pale. I think it is special to be an albino, and I usually don't regret it. A lot of people compliment me on my light hair. I like the attention!

Another way I get attention is by showing my skills in playing the piano and singing. I have enjoyed these talents since I was young, and I may even pursue a career in these areas.

I am fun-loving, a hard worker, somewhat even-tempered, and friendly. And one thing I will never forget is to like myself for what I am.

*Kirstin Schreiber
Grade 6*

I was born in Palm Beach, Florida, on March 12, 1983. I became diabetic when I was six years old. I find balancing my sugar a challenge, but my motto is to control it and not let it beat me.

Even though I have diabetes, I like to be active. I play tennis, swim, and love to go snorkeling in the warm Caribbean. I also spend a lot of my free time reading and playing on my computer.

*Christopher Keith Temple
Grade 3*

I'M EXTRA SPECIAL!

What makes me different is the way I don't try to act or look like the people who are popular. My friends are few, but true.

I am a talented young lady. I'm a competitive swimmer, a violinist, an honor student, a member of a youth symphony, and a teenager with epilepsy.

If I had to narrow down the one thing that makes me different it would be my epilepsy. I have to take medication, go to bed earlier than other people my age, and be more aware of what's happening within me. I also have to be more cautious than other people — I can't get overworked or overtired. Epilepsy isn't something you can see, but it influences me greatly.

Sarah Higgins
Grade 8

My name is Joseph and I am 12 years old. I am an asthmatic, but that doesn't hold me down. I am very active in sports and enjoy baseball and football most of all. During the football season I play defensive linebacker and offensive guard. In Little League my position is catcher. I chose this position to help me with my fear of getting up to bat!

One hot day after practice, I had to go to the doctor because of an asthma attack. After two injections of adrenaline (which didn't help), I had to go to the hospital for a few days. As soon as I came home, I went right back to catching in the Little League. I couldn't let my team down! As you can see, I am a very determined person!

Joey Fantozzi
Grade 7

I'm going to talk about something that happened to me. I take this very seriously, and I also like people to know about it.

I was born three months premature and I had a problem — my fingers weren't fully developed. When I was born I had six fingers on my left hand and four fingers on my right. The extra finger on the left was meant to be on my right, but it didn't work out.

I have had a total of eight surgeries, but they have not been

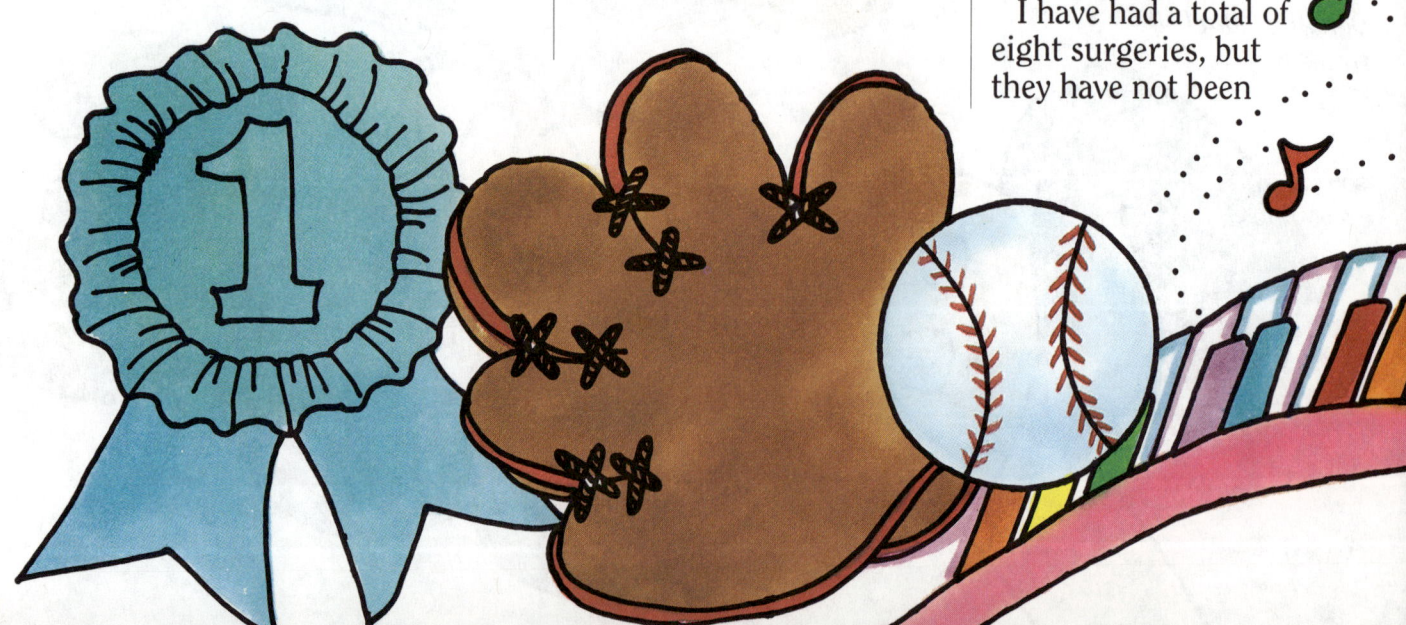

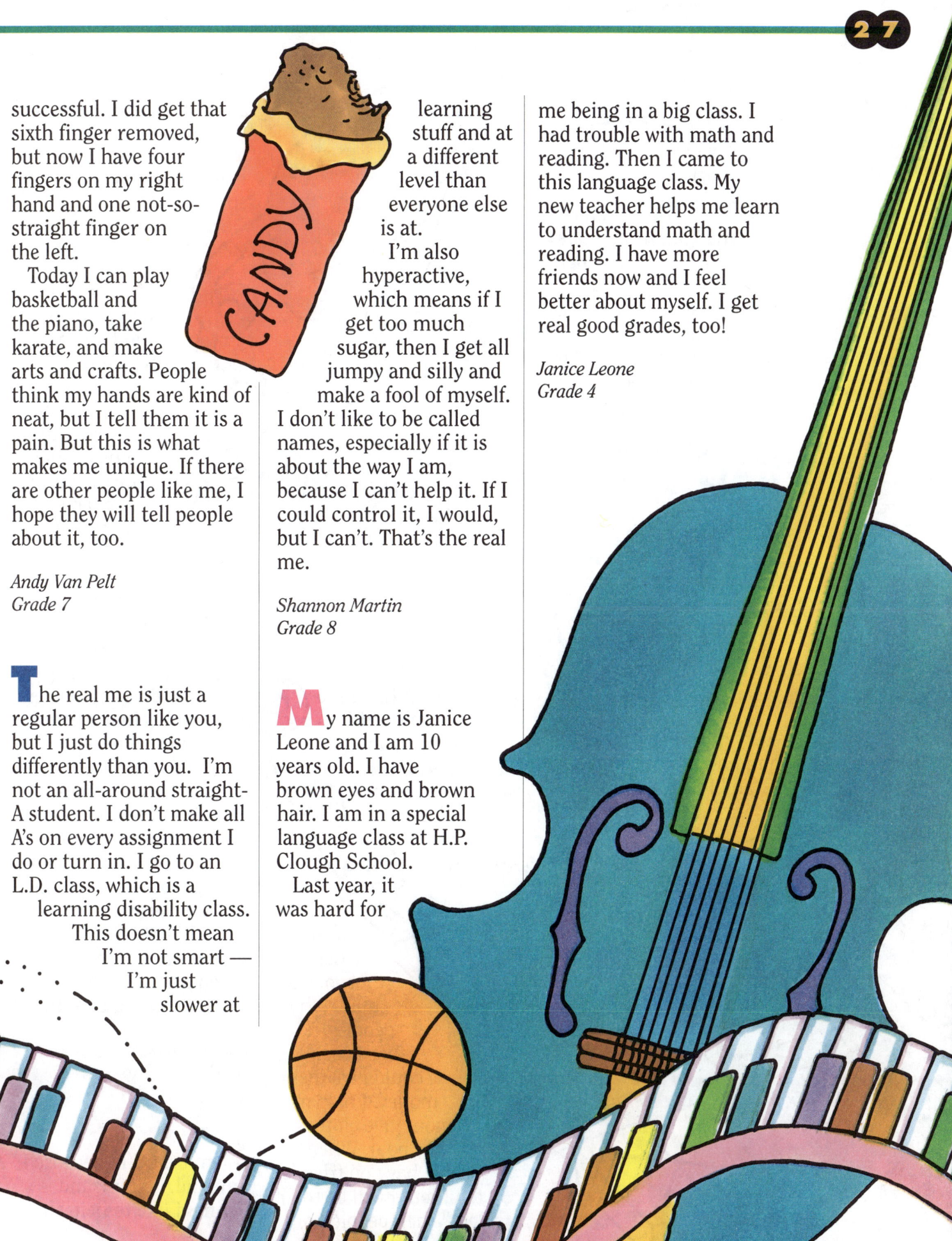

successful. I did get that sixth finger removed, but now I have four fingers on my right hand and one not-so-straight finger on the left.

Today I can play basketball and the piano, take karate, and make arts and crafts. People think my hands are kind of neat, but I tell them it is a pain. But this is what makes me unique. If there are other people like me, I hope they will tell people about it, too.

Andy Van Pelt
Grade 7

The real me is just a regular person like you, but I just do things differently than you. I'm not an all-around straight-A student. I don't make all A's on every assignment I do or turn in. I go to an L.D. class, which is a learning disability class. This doesn't mean I'm not smart — I'm just slower at learning stuff and at a different level than everyone else is at.

I'm also hyperactive, which means if I get too much sugar, then I get all jumpy and silly and make a fool of myself. I don't like to be called names, especially if it is about the way I am, because I can't help it. If I could control it, I would, but I can't. That's the real me.

Shannon Martin
Grade 8

My name is Janice Leone and I am 10 years old. I have brown eyes and brown hair. I am in a special language class at H.P. Clough School.

Last year, it was hard for me being in a big class. I had trouble with math and reading. Then I came to this language class. My new teacher helps me learn to understand math and reading. I have more friends now and I feel better about myself. I get real good grades, too!

Janice Leone
Grade 4

Kind And Caring — That's Me!

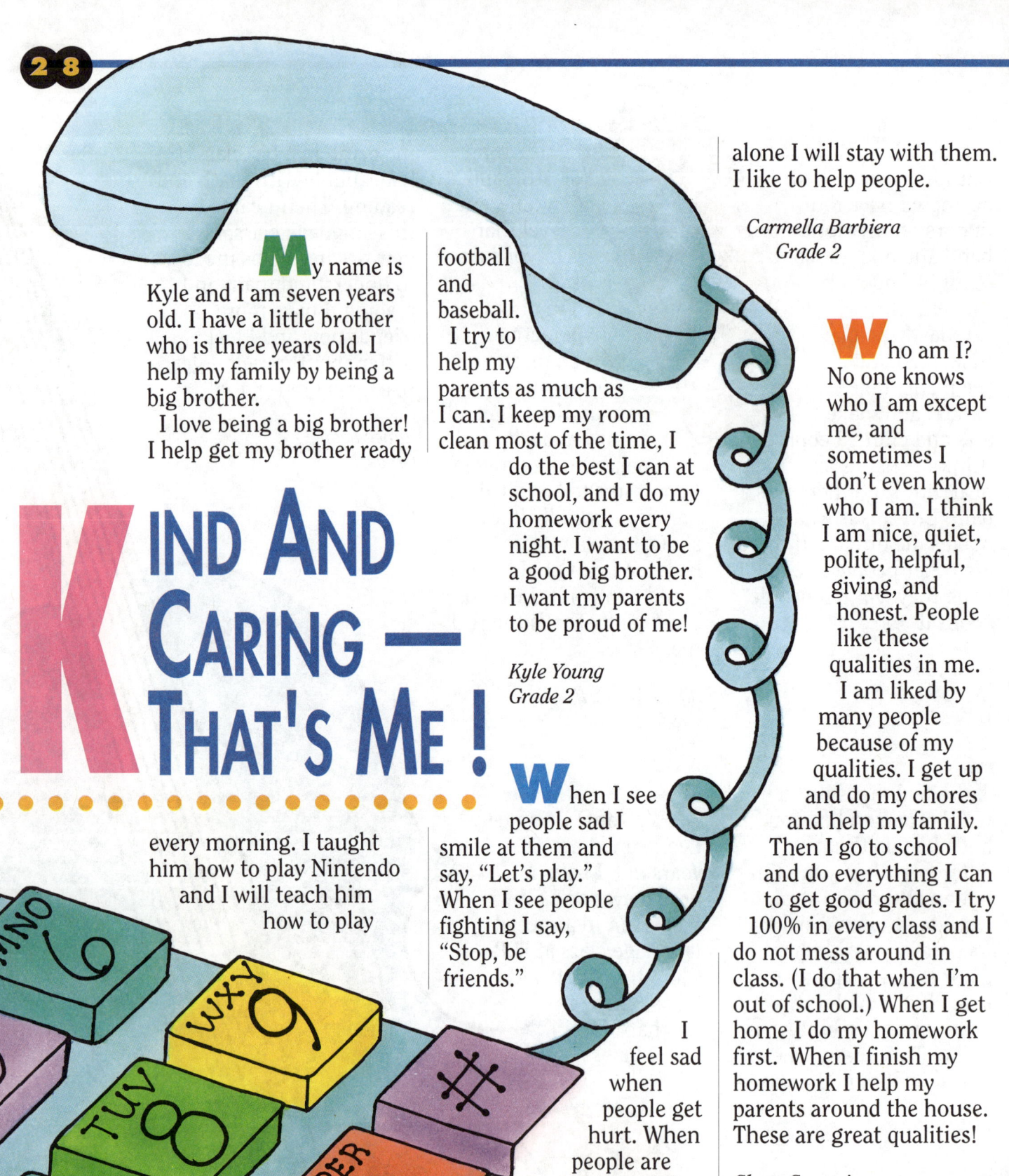

My name is Kyle and I am seven years old. I have a little brother who is three years old. I help my family by being a big brother.

I love being a big brother! I help get my brother ready every morning. I taught him how to play Nintendo and I will teach him how to play football and baseball.

I try to help my parents as much as I can. I keep my room clean most of the time, I do the best I can at school, and I do my homework every night. I want to be a good big brother. I want my parents to be proud of me!

Kyle Young
Grade 2

When I see people sad I smile at them and say, "Let's play." When I see people fighting I say, "Stop, be friends."

I feel sad when people get hurt. When people are poor I wish I could give them money. I help my mom give clothes to the poor. When people have no friends I tell them I will be their friend. When people are alone I will stay with them. I like to help people.

Carmella Barbiera
Grade 2

Who am I? No one knows who I am except me, and sometimes I don't even know who I am. I think I am nice, quiet, polite, helpful, giving, and honest. People like these qualities in me.

I am liked by many people because of my qualities. I get up and do my chores and help my family. Then I go to school and do everything I can to get good grades. I try 100% in every class and I do not mess around in class. (I do that when I'm out of school.) When I get home I do my homework first. When I finish my homework I help my parents around the house. These are great qualities!

Chase Cummings
Grade 8

I am beautiful because I am kind, helpful, and loving. I like to help all kinds of people. Some ways I am helpful are: playing with my brother when my mom is busy, helping the kids in my class understand math, and other things. I show my mom how much I love her by drawing pictures for her, giving her hugs and kisses, and keeping my room clean. I like to be kind by taking flowers to my teacher to make her smile and by calling my grandma on the phone just to say "Hi."

*Erika Fletcher
Grade 2*

I am a boy and my name is Ty Osborne. I weigh fifty pounds. I have a big imagination. I live with my mom and dad in a trailer park that my dad owns. I have seven cousins, 27 aunts and uncles, 37 friends, a dog named Freckles, three ducks, and three horses.

I have a nice teacher and I love the American flag. I take out the garbage, clean the dog, take the dog for a walk, and help set the table when my mom tells me to.

*Ty Osborne
Grade 3*

Very few kids try to accept those children with mental disabilities. I think I am special because in second grade, I did try.

It all started with a physical education class in which I was paired up with a mentally disabled girl. After class, I realized this girl was just like me, but lonely.

Soon after our meeting, I requested time to help in the special education classes during recess. I was denied permission at first, but I persisted, and finally my request was accepted. Even today I love my special friends.

*Emily C. DePrang
Grade 6*

Now I Know The Real Me

I was a small boy at heart. I kept on searching for myself, but I couldn't find the "real me." Finally, I found myself. I wanted to be a violinist. It was my wildest dream. When I started to tell everyone, they shot me down. They made fun of me. It really made me feel bad. I had finally found my dream, yet they shot me down like a plane in Vietnam. It was horrible. I felt like I was the loneliest human being alive.

The first eight years of my life were like that. But as I got older I started to think and make mature decisions. It really made a difference in my life. I think my life has changed so much since then. And oh, my violin dream is coming true!

Christopher S. Beale
Grade 7

There's an old saying that goes something like, "Don't try to be like someone else. Just be yourself — that's all that matters." Enjoy life, stay off drugs, stay in school, and you'll be a real person — a real you! And be proud of yourself and your interests. There's only one you and me, and we're special — more than anyone could say.

Stephaine Vezina
Grade 7

In my eyes, I see myself as a well thought-out painting. A splatter of honesty, a line of friendliness, a brush of intelligence, and maybe just a dot of self pride. In 1977 when this painting was created, it was every spectator's dream to accomplish a work of art just like it. Now, this painting is even better and more unique than ever.

I, Samantha Pino, am proud of who I am. Someday I hope to be as wonderful as the people who made me what I am — my parents. I thank them for giving me the courage to "never say never" and to always follow my dreams. And that's just what I plan to do: fulfill the greatness of the real me.

Samantha Pino
Grade 8

A SPECIAL THANKS TO:

Aiello, Vanessa, *Grade 2,*
Horace Mann School,
North Bergen, NJ

Annarelli, Dan, *Grade 7,*
St. Denis School, Havertown, PA

Austin, Michael, *Grade 2,*
Sullivans School, Yokosuka, Japan

Babadzhanov, Vlad, *Grade 6,*
RASG Hebrew Academy,
Miami Beach, FL

Barber, Kelly, *Grade 2,*
Ebenezer School, Statesville, NC

Barbiera, Carmella, *Grade 2,*
St. Teresa School, Staten Island, NY

Barrett, Moses, *Grade 2,*
The Learning Workshop,
Forest Grove, OR

Beale, Christopher S., *Grade 7,*
Academy for Academics and Arts,
Huntsville, AL

Bemah, Willimena, *Grade 2,*
Leimbach Elementary,
Sacramento, CA

Berghorn, Ed, *Grade 4,*
Akron Elementary, Akron, NY

Blankenship, Justin, *Grade 5,*
Crystal Springs Middle School,
Crystal Springs, MS

Burbage, Ronnie, *Grade 5,*
James B. Edwards Elementary,
Mt. Pleasant, SC

Burritt, Meaghan, *Grade 6,*
Lakeshore Junior High School,
Stevensville, MI

Carro, Joseph, *Grade 3,*
St. Andrew Avellino School,
Flushing, NY

Clacko, Mary, *Grade 3,*
Haine School, Mars, PA

Clemons, Melony, *Grade 7,*
Academy for Academics and Arts,
Huntsville, AL

Coburn, Dan, *Grade 4,*
Morgan School, Beloit, WI

Como, Christine, *Grade 3,*
St. Andrew Avellino School,
Flushing, NY

Cook, David, *Grade 2,*
Lake Elementary School,
Pascagoula, MS

Crabtrey, Kena, *Grade 6,*
Rehobeth School, Dothan, AL

Cummings, Chase, *Grade 8,*
St. Maria Goretti School,
Arlington, TX

Dalton, Mary, *Grade 7,*
Roosevelt Junior High School,
Altoona, PA

DeFrancesco, Anthony, *Grade 5,*
E.T. Richardson Middle School,
Springfield, PA

DePrang, Emily C., *Grade 6,*
Jamison Middle School,
Pearland, TX

Diaz, Lourdes, *Grade 8,*
Academia Maria Reina, Rio Piedras,
Puerto Rico

DiStefano, Vinnie, *Grade 4,*
Jefferson School, Bergenfield, NJ

Eddy, Raymond, *Grade 6,*
King Intermediate School,
King, NC

Elia, Katie, *Grade 6,*
Glen Landing Middle School,
Blackwood, NJ

Fantozzi, Joey, *Grade 7,*
Secaucus Middle School,
Secaucus, NJ

Findley, Blaine, *Grade 8,*
Carver Middle School, Century, FL

Fletcher, Erika, *Grade 2,*
Jack Harvey School,
Sterling Heights, MI

Gerossie, Colleen, *Grade 2,*
Swallow-Union School,
Dunstable, MA

Harris, Missy, *Grade 4,*
St. Clement School, Cincinnati, OH

Higgins, Sarah, *Grade 8,*
St. Paul's School, St. Petersburg, FL

Hinkle, James, *Grade 6,*
Christian Way School, Aurora, CO

Holman, Heather, *Grade 5,*
Madison Area Junior High School,
Madison, ME

Humphrey, Misti C., *Grade 8,*
Canutillo Middle School,
Canutillo, TX

Jacobs, Kelley, *Grade 8,*
Marengo Academy, Linden, AL

Jett, Talton, *Grade 2,*
Our Lady Star of the Sea School,
New Orleans, LA

Kenoyer, Gwuinifer, *Grade 5,*
El Dorado School, Lancaster, CA

Kimble, Jennifer, *Grade 2,*
Franklin Elementary, Franklin, WV

Klein, Anne, *Grade 7,*
Mason Middle School, Mason, MI

Koscica, Anthony, *Grade 3,*
St. Andrew Avellino School,
Flushing, NY

Le, Tram, *Grade 5,*
Anza School, El Cajon, CA

Leone, Janice, *Grade 4,*
H.P. Clough School, Mendon, MA

Lyman, Ricky, *Grade 4,*
Lena Whitmore Elementary,
Moscow, ID

Maldonado, Arturo, *Grade 5,*
Stockton School, Chicago, IL

Mantilla, Rober, *Grade 7,*
Secaucus Middle School,
Secaucus, NJ

Martin, Shannon, *Grade 8,*
Wood Middle School, Ft. Wood, MO

Mitchell, Don Allen, *Grade 8,*
Greenfield High School,
Greenfield, MO

Mitry, Daniel, *Grade 7,*
Reading-Fleming Middle School,
Flemington, NJ

Murray, Bronwen, *Grade 7,*
Academy for Academics and Arts,
Huntsville, AL

Osborne, Ty, *Grade 3,*
Krebs School, Krebs, OK

Parulis, Lisa, *Grade 7,*
Ramblewood Middle School,
Coral Springs, FL

Passaloukos, Steve, *Grade 5,*
Edgar L. Miller School,
Merrillville, IN

Patterson, Lexy, *Grade 6,*
Pacific Union College Elementary,
Angwin, CA

Pino, Samantha, *Grade 8,*
Glen Landing Middle School,
Blackwood, NJ

Radford, Tara, *Grade 2,*
Stuarts Draft Elementary,
Stuarts Draft, VA

Rapp, B.J., *Grade 7,*
Powell Middle School, Littleton, CO

Restivo, Alan, *Grade 2,*
La Vace Stewart Elementary,
Kemah, TX

Reyburn, Justin, *Grade 6,*
St. Maria Goretti School,
Arlington, TX

Royster, Taquanica L., *Grade 4,*
C.G. Credle School, Oxford, NC

Ruud, Derek, *Grade 8,*
Grygla Junior High School,
Grygla, MN

Saxe, Jennifer, *Grade 4,*
Anna P. Mote School,
Wilmington, DE

Schaeffer, Kevin, *Grade 7,*
Armstrong East Junior High
School, Dayton, PA

Schreiber, Kirstin, *Grade 6,*
Greenville Middle School,
Greenville, NC

Silva, Alberto, *Grade 8,*
St. Francis Xavier School,
Waterbury, CT

Siple, Kristin, *Grade 8,*
Oak Bluffs School, Oak Bluffs, MA

Stark, Leah, *Grade 6,*
Carroll County Middle School,
Carrollton, KY

Suriano, Patricia, *Grade 5,*
Colegio Maya,
Guatemala City, Guatemala

Swain, Spencer, *Grade 5,*
Sandy Hook School, Sandy Hook, CT

Temple, Christopher Keith, *Grade 3,*
Antilles School, St. Thomas,
U.S. Virgin Islands

Theodossiou, John, *Grade 7,*
Antietam Junior/Senior High School,
Reading, PA

Tracy, Killeen, *Grade 7,*
Fields Memorial School, Bozrah, CT

Van Pelt, Andy, *Grade 7,*
St. Pius X School, Portland, OR

Vezina, Stephaine, *Grade 7,*
Home School, Middleburg, FL

Virk, Gurpreet, *Grade 3,*
Yamato Colony School, Livingston,
CA

Wang, Fifi, *Grade 2,*
Beitel Elementary, Laramie, WY

White, Ronda, *Grade 6,*
Mill Creek Grade School,
Peck's Mill, WV

Williams, Jeanine, *Grade 6,*
P.S. 225, Rockaway Park, NY

Yogarajah, Nadhira, *Grade 7,*
Christ the King School, Yonkers, NY

Young, Kyle, *Grade 2,*
Kidwell Elementary, Iowa Park, TX